DATE DUE NOV 05

GAYLORD			PRINTED IN U.S.A.

A YOUNG RIDER'S GUIDE
LEARN TO RIDE

A YOUNG RIDER'S GUIDE
LEARN TO RIDE

Carolyn Henderson
Foreword by Lynn Russell

DK Publishing, Inc.

LONDON, NEW YORK, MUNICH,
MELBOURNE, and DELHI

Project Editor Claire Bampton **Project Art Editor** Lesley Betts
Series Editor Maggie Crowley **Series Art Editor** Sharon Grant
Editor Kathleen Bada **Designer** Darren Holt
U.S. Editors Connie Robinson and Sharon Lemon

DTP Designer Nomazwe Madonko
Photographers Andy Crawford and John Henderson
Production Lisa Moss **Picture Researcher** Francis Vargo
Jacket design Margherita Gianni

Managing Editor Jayne Parsons
Managing Art Editor Gill Shaw

First published in the United States in 1999 by
DK Publishing, Inc.
375 Hudson Street, New York, New York 10014
as *Improve Your Riding Skills* ISBN 0-7894-4264-7 (hardcover) 0-7894-4263-9 (paperback)
This edition published in 2005

05 06 07 08 09 10 9 8 7 6 5 4 3 2 1

A catalog record for this book is
available from the Library of Congress.
ISBN 0-7566-1449-X

Color reproduction by Colourscan, Singapore
Printed and bound in China by SNP Leefung

Discover more at
www.dk.com

CONTENTS

FOREWORD

LEARNING TO RIDE is exciting and fun. Whatever you hope to do, whether it is trail riding, jumping or, like me, competing in top-level show classes, it is important to learn the skills step by step. This book will take you from your first lessons on a lead rein to the stage where you are ready to own or share a pony. You'll also learn about handling and taking care of ponies safely, and find out how to help train a pony and deal with any problems you encounter.

Lynn Russell

LYNN RUSSELL
TOP SHOW RIDER

GETTING STARTED

THE BEST PLACE to learn to ride a pony is at a good riding stable. Here there are experienced trainers who have learned how to work with novice riders. These trainers are familiar with the most suitable horses and ponies on which to learn, so your lessons will be safe and enjoyable. Try to take a lesson at least once a week – more often if you have the chance.

Instructor leads pony while you ride.

Ready to ride

Dress safely and comfortably for your lessons. Always wear a hat or helmet that meets the highest safety standards. Many stables will lend you one at first, but eventually you will need to buy your own. Never buy a secondhand hat, since it may have been damaged in a fall. Jodhpurs or comfortable pants and riding boots or safe shoes are also essential.

Hat must fit properly.

YOUR TRAINER
During the first few lessons, your trainer will lead your pony using either a lead rein or a long lunge rein. This allows you to concentrate on sitting correctly and getting used to the feel of riding.

Always fasten the safety harness.

Horse should be in good condition – neither too fat nor too thin.

Tack should fit the horse well and be correctly adjusted.

Stirrup irons must be the correct size, so your feet cannot slide through or become trapped.

Long rubber riding boots or short jodhpur boots are suitable for beginners.

THE RIGHT PONY
Your trainer will choose a horse or pony for your lessons that is the right size for you. It should be quiet, friendly, and reliable and be used to being ridden and handled by beginners.

Horse should be well shod.

Choosing a riding stable

Friends who are also learning to ride may recommend suitable stables. Local vets, tack shop employees, and pony club officers may also have addresses of suitable establishments. Visit a stable before arranging for any lessons and check that it seems well run. Horses should be in good condition and the staff friendly and helpful.

THE STABLE

The grounds should be neat, with tools and equipment stored safely. There should be an enclosed riding arena. Some schools may also have indoor arenas.

Ponies must have shelter from bad weather and shade from heat when tied up.

Trainer should check tack before rider mounts.

Check that stables and buildings are in good condition.

Riding school ponies are usually older, experienced animals. They must not be lame.

TACKING UP

TACK UP IN A STABLE, or outside with a halter fastened around the horse's neck so that you have control over it. Try to be gentle and quiet when you tack up, so that the horse remains calm. Make sure that the tack is safe and check it regularly for loose stitching or cracked leather.

Place your right hand on the horse's nose to give more control.

Putting on a bridle

Before you start to put on a bridle, make sure the noseband and throatlatch are undone. Put the reins over the horse's head, remove the halter, and fasten it around the horse's neck to prevent it from walking away.

1 Bit in mouth
Slide your left thumb into the corner of the horse's mouth and gently guide the bit in.

Treat ears with care.

2 Over the ears
Put the headstall over the horse's ears and place the ears through the gap between the headstall and browband. Try not to pinch the ears. Take the forelock out from under the browband.

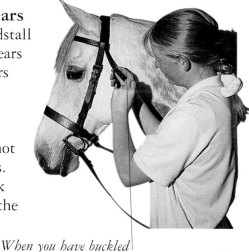

3 Fastening straps
Fasten the noseband and throatlatch. Once fastened, you should be able to fit a hand's width between the throatlatch and horse's face, and two fingers between the noseband and face.

Check that the bit fits comfortably. If it is too low in the mouth, it could hit against the horse's teeth.

When you have buckled up the throatlatch, check that it fits correctly.

Taking off a bridle

Before removing the bridle, make sure the horse is secure with a halter around its neck. Then unfasten the noseband and throatlatch, bring the reins to the poll, and slide the bridle and reins forward and off. Wait for the horse to release the bit from its mouth, or the bit may get caught or bang on its teeth.

Bring the reins to the poll.

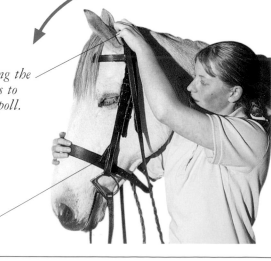

Check that the noseband and throatlatch are undone.

Putting on a saddle

First check that the stirrup irons are run up, the saddle pad is in place, and the girth is folded over the saddle.

Girth folded over saddle.

1 In position
Lower the saddle gently over withers and slide back into position so coat hairs lie flat.

2 Fastening girth
Pull saddle pad up into the saddle. Carefully release girth so that it dangles down. Reach under the horse's belly for the girth, and fasten it. You should be able to slide your fingers between the girth and the horse.

Fasten one buckle at a time.

Taking off a saddle

Take off your saddle with as much care as you put it on. Once you remove the saddle, put it where it will not get damaged.

Place leathers between stirrups and saddle.

1 Run up stirrups
First run the stirrups up the leathers so they do not bang against the horse. Undo the girth.

2 Remove saddle
Place the girth over the saddle. The outside of the girth should be facing away from the saddle, so that any dried mud does not scratch it. Carefully lift off the saddle.

Lift saddle from horse's back.

All tacked up
Once tacking up is finished, check all fastenings and see that the tack fits correctly. The bit should be high enough to fit snugly into the corners of the mouth. Straighten the bit, noseband, and browband if necessary. Tighten the girth, then gently pull each foreleg forward to release any wrinkled skin.

Saddle must not pinch withers.

The stirrups should always be run up when you are not riding.

The girth should be tight enough to stop the saddle from sliding.

If leaving the horse tied up, twist reins under the throatlatch.

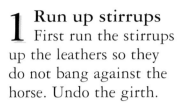

WELL-FITTED SADDLE
A horse can only work well if its tack fits and is comfortable. The tree, or frame, of a saddle must be the correct width. A properly fitted saddle will not pinch, rub, or interfere with the horse's movement.

MOUNTING AND DISMOUNTING

ONE OF THE FIRST things you learn when riding is how to get on and off a pony. One way to mount is to put one foot in the stirrup and to jump up. You can also mount by standing on a mounting block, or by asking for a leg up. There are also different ways to dismount.

Landing heavily may cause the pony discomfort.

Mounting
Before you begin, make sure the girth is tight enough to stop the saddle from sliding around. Most riders mount from the left side, facing the horse's tail.

Leg clears pony's back.

Keep reins short so that the pony does not move forward.

Stand with your left shoulder next to the pony's left shoulder.

2 Lowering into saddle
Swing your right leg over the pony's back, being careful not to kick the pony. Gently lower yourself into the saddle.

Sit straight in the saddle.

1 Foot in the stirrup
Turn the back edge of the stirrup toward you, place your left foot in it, and jump up off your right foot.

3 In the saddle
Slip your right foot into the stirrup. Take up a light feel on the reins and sit up tall. Check your girth before you ride off.

Dismounting

Get off with as much care and consideration as you used to get on. You may need to ask someone to help you if you are getting off a young or difficult pony.

Lean forward to start the swing down.

Keep reins short so that you are in control of the pony.

Try to avoid kicking or prodding the pony as you dismount.

1 Start of dismount
Take both feet out of the stirrups, lean forward, and swing your right leg carefully over the pony's back.

Swing right leg over pony's back.

Bend your knees as you land on the ground.

2 Jumping down
Let yourself down in a quiet, smooth jump without pulling the saddle over. Try to keep your balance as you land.

Alternative dismounting

Some riders keep one foot in the stirrup as they dismount. Take your right foot out of the stirrup and swing your leg over the horse's back. Keep your weight over the horse's withers. When your legs are parallel, slip your left foot from the stirrup and jump down to the ground. Always dismount in the way that your trainer tells you.

In Australia, riders dismount by keeping one foot in the stirrup.

IN THE SADDLE

LESSONS ON THE LUNGE or lead rein will get you used to the feel of sitting on a moving horse. Your trainer will help you achieve the correct position so that you and your horse are well balanced. You will also learn to give your horse clear instructions, called aids, with your legs, hands, and body weight. If you give the correct aids, and your horse is well trained, you will soon feel in control.

Hold the reins slightly apart, with your thumbs on top.

HOLDING THE REINS
Hold the reins in both hands, so that they pass between your little and ring fingers, through your palms, and out between your index fingers and thumbs.

Your first lesson
Your first lesson is usually on the lunge and may be spent mainly at the walk, though you may be able to try a few trotting strides. Your instructor will control the horse, so you can concentrate on your riding technique. Do not worry if there seems to be a lot to remember – it becomes easier with practice.

Keep your arms relaxed.

Ask the horse to walk by squeezing its sides equally with both legs.

Contact with the horse's mouth should be light, not pulling back.

A horse on a lunge rein travels in a circle.

FIRST LESSON

- Feel the horse's mouth without pulling on the reins

- Look ahead, not down

- There should be a straight (perpendicular) line through your shoulder, elbow, hip, and heel

- Think about absorbing the horse's movements through your lower back

- Think about sitting tall but staying supple

- Stirrups should stay under the widest part of your foot

During one of your first lessons, you may be taught how to tighten the girth. To do this, hold the reins in your right hand and swing your left leg forward. Lift the saddle flap with your left hand and tighten the girth. You should be able to fit the flat of your fingers between the girth and the horse.

Adjust the buckles one at a time.

A horse may expand its belly as you tighten the girth, so check it again after a few minutes.

ADJUSTING STIRRUP LEATHERS
To adjust the stirrup leathers, hold the reins in one hand and pull the stirrup leather out and down, keeping your foot in the stirrup. Slide the buckle prong into the correct hole and pull the stirrup leather back up so the buckle is at the top again.

Markers are used for more complicated exercises in later lessons.

The riding arena should be a safe, enclosed area.

Keep your toes pointing forward and your heels down.

Keep your foot in the stirrup while you adjust the length of the stirrup leather.

The trainer controls your horse so you can concentrate on sitting correctly and getting used to the feel of a moving horse.

15

THE FIRST STEPS

WHEN YOU HAVE LEARNED how to sit on a horse at the walk, you will be ready to learn to control your horse's direction and speed by yourself. To communicate with a horse, give it signals with your legs, seat, hands, and voice. These are called the natural aids and will be used first of all to start, stop, and turn.

Voice

Hands

Sit tall, without bracing your back.

Seat

Reins should not be tight or hang in loops.

Legs

Starting off
Before moving off, check that your stirrups are the correct length and that your girth is tight enough. Your legs should rest lightly against the horse's sides and your reins should be at a length that gives a light contact with the horse's mouth, without pulling.

THE AIDS
The aids are signals that a horse is trained to understand. For example, a gentle squeeze of the legs means walk forward, and closing the fingers on the reins means stop. Stop giving the aid as soon as the horse obeys, or it will become confused.

Straight line from elbows through hands to horse's mouth

Feel the side-to-side movement in the seat.

1 Using the natural aids
Look ahead and close both legs gently against the horse's sides. Stop squeezing as soon as it walks forward. If there is no response, pause, then squeeze a little harder.

2 Starting the walk
Allow your hands to follow the movement of the horse's head, so contact with its mouth is light and flexible.

The Walk

The walk has a 1-2-3-4 rhythm. The sequence of steps is left hind, left fore, right hind, and finally right fore. The horse always has at least two feet on the ground at any one time. A horse naturally has a long walk stride and a relaxed neck.

Try not to restrict the walk when riding the horse.

Right hind leg is followed by right foreleg.

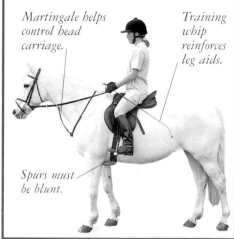

Artificial aids

Experienced riders may use equipment such as whips, spurs, and martingales to give signals. These are called artificial aids and must be used with care. Whips and spurs must never be used to hurt a horse and should not be used by beginners.

Martingale helps control head carriage.

Training whip reinforces leg aids.

Spurs must be blunt.

Sitting tall and still helps to slow down horse.

Ears back and relaxed means horse is paying attention to rider.

Horse should stay relaxed through neck and mouth.

Outside leg is behind the girth to stop horse's hind-quarters from swinging out.

Wrists should be supple and straight.

3 **To stop the horse**
To halt, sit tall and tighten your seat and thigh muscles. Close your fingers on the reins without pulling back. Keep your legs in contact with the horse's sides to keep the horse balanced.

Halt should be square with legs together.

Turning

When turning, look where you want to go, so that you position your weight correctly. To turn left, squeeze gently on the left rein and also with the left leg. Allow the right rein to loosen slightly so the horse's head can turn. Don't try to turn sharply.

TROTTING

A HORSE HAS four gaits — walk, trot, canter, and gallop — and you will learn about each in turn. Trot can be ridden sitting, when the movement is absorbed through the rider's lower back, or rising, when the rider sits and rises in time with the horse's stride. Both become easier with practice.

Start by riding on the right diagonal.

Sit for one beat, then rise again to change diagonals.

Left hind foot and right forefoot touch down together.

DIAGONALS
Changing diagonals switches the position of the rider's weight. This makes riding easier for the horse, just like switching a heavy object from hand to hand makes it easier for you to carry. To change diagonals, sit for one beat, then rise again.

Learning to trot
Most riders spend more time in rising trot than in sitting trot. This is because as long as the rider is balanced and does not bump up and down, rising is more comfortable for the horse and easier for the rider. Western riders sit to a slow trot, called a jog.

Bend elbows slightly to maintain light rein contact.

1 Moving forward
To move forward from a walk to a rising trot, close your legs against the horse's side in a quick inward squeeze. Hold the reins to allow a light contact with the horse's mouth.

Close both legs on horse's side with a quick, inward nudge.

Walk should be active before asking for trot.

Legs move in diagonal pairs.

The trot

The trot is a two-time gait in which the legs move in diagonal pairs. The right (offside) foreleg and left (nearside) hind leg move forward at the same time in a 1-2, 1-2 rhythm. A trotting horse naturally moves in balance, with rhythmic strides.

Only one foreleg or hind leg bears the horse's weight at any one time.

Hock joints provide power to push horse forward.

Rise in a slightly forward, not upward, position.

2 Rising up into trot
Let the horse's stride push you slightly forward and out of the saddle. Do not grip with your knees or try to stand in the stirrups.

Horse's movement pushes you out of the saddle.

Move back into saddle as gently as possible.

3 Sitting down
Sink back into the saddle and let the horse's movement push you forward and out again. Counting the 1-2, 1-2 rhythm of the trot out loud might help.

Rider's knee and ankle joints absorbs her weight.

Right foreleg and left hind leg move forward together.

19

EXERCISES IN THE SADDLE

EXERCISES IN AND OUT of the saddle will help you become confident and supple when riding. It is important that the horse on which you practice mounted exercises is quiet and safe, and that your trainer is in control. Riding without stirrups will improve your balance and can be done on or off the lunge line. Ride without stirrups only in safe surroundings – not on the road or trail. The more relaxed and confident you become, the more your horse will trust you and your riding will improve.

This exercise improves your agility and tones your thigh and stomach muscles.

Swing right leg over withers, taking care not to touch the horse.

Trainer holds horse so that it remains still during the exercise.

Around-the-world

Before starting this exercise, remove the stirrups or cross them in front of the saddle so that they are out of the way. This exercise is easier to perform in an anticlockwise direction. Swing your right leg over the horse's withers to sit sideways, then swing your left leg over the quarters to face the tail. Continue until you are facing forward again.

Keep your leg stretched downward as you swing the other leg over the withers or hindquarters.

Without stirrups

Riding without stirrups is an excellent way to improve your balance and helps you absorb the horse's movement through your lower back. This exercise is especially good for improving your sitting trot. Start off by riding without stirrups for short periods, then rest.

Side reins control horse's head carriage when it is on the lunge.

Allow your legs to stretch down without gripping with your knees.

Forward stretch

This exercise helps you improve your balance. While walking, bend forward from the hip and stretch out your arms toward the horse's ears. Try to keep your lower leg in the correct position, without moving it too far forward or back.

Some horses dislike having their ears touched, so stretch forward without actually touching the horse.

This exercise is practiced when the horse is walking or standing still.

A moving horse must be controlled by a trainer.

Getting in shape

There are lots of ways to improve your fitness and suppleness, even when you are unable to ride. Swimming is excellent for allover exercise and uses many of the muscles you use when riding. Biking and skipping are also beneficial for building leg muscles. Increase exercise times gradually or you may end up with aching muscles! Floor exercises such as the ones shown here may also help.

Jump up into the air and stretch upward as far as you can.

Start off in a squatting position with your hands at your sides.

Swing each leg forward and backward from the hip to loosen muscles.

CANTERING AND GALLOPING

THE CANTER AND THE GALLOP are faster than the trot. The gallop is the fastest gait of all and when galloping you must stay in complete control. During a gallop, bend forward from the hips so that your weight is just out of the saddle and is absorbed by your knees and ankles. During a canter, sit upright but remain relaxed, and absorb the horse's movement through your lower back.

Sit upright, but remain relaxed and look ahead.

Horse takes a longer stride with its right leg.

THE LEADING LEG
A cantering horse takes a longer stride with one foreleg than the other. This is called the leading leg. On a circle or bend, the correct leading leg is the inside leg – for example, in a clockwise circle, the right leg leads.

Preparing to canter
Before you ask a horse to canter, establish a balanced but active trot. It is easier to get the correct leading leg (also called the lead) by asking for a canter when you are trotting in a circle or in one corner of the arena.

1 Ask for canter
Maintain an active trot without rushing. Sit for one or two strides, then brush your outside leg slightly behind the horse's girth. At the same time nudge your inside leg near the horse's girth.

Trot should be active before you "ask for the canter".

2 The canter
Try not to restrict the horse's head and neck as it moves into the canter. Sit tall but remain relaxed, and keep your lower back supple to absorb the movement.

Keep contact with the horse's mouth.

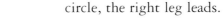

Galloping

Once you can canter properly, you can learn to gallop. Instead of keeping your seat as you do for a canter, bend forward from the hips and shift your weight just out of the saddle. Only gallop in safe surroundings where the visibility and terrain are good. You should be in control of the pace, not the horse. The gallop has a 1,2,3,4 four-beat gait.

Maintain a forward position.

Shorten stirrups by one or two holes to make it easier to stay balanced.

Cantering gait

A canter has a 1,2,3 three-beat gait. When the horse's right leg leads, the left hind foot falls first, then the right hind foot and the left forefoot together, then the right forefoot.

Hindquarters provide power.

Horse's neck stretches as speed increases.

Use your weight distribution and the rein to give the horse a "slow down" signal.

3 Slowing down
To return to a trot, sit up and tighten your thigh and seat muscles. At the same time, close your fingers on the reins without pulling back.

4 Back to a trot
As the horse moves into a trot, relax your fingers on the reins. Sit for one stride, then move forward into a rising trot.

Changing pace is called making a transition.

A trot is often more energetic just after the horse has cantered.

MAKING PROGRESS

YOUR FIRST LESSONS will be given to you one-on-one by a trainer, but as you gain confidence you will probably join a group lesson with other new riders. During the group lessons you will learn how to control your horse around other horses, and how to perform different exercises in the schooling arena. You will develop your knowledge of aids to communicate more effectively with your horse.

Right rein allows the horse to turn.

Left rein instructs the horse which direction to follow.

USING THE CORRECT AIDS
Your trainer will help you develop a more detailed knowledge of how to use the aids. For example, to turn left, look left, squeeze the left rein, and release the right rein slightly. At the same time, close your left leg on the horse's side and move your right leg back to control the angle of the hindquarters.

Group lessons
Your group will contain up to five or six riders. Riding in a group teaches you to be aware of other horses and their riders. Always keep a safe distance from the horse in front, since it might kick.

The first rider is called the leader.

Make sure you do not bump into the horse in front.

Passing side by side

When you pass another horse and rider, you need to make sure that you do not bump into them. The easiest way to do this is to pass so that your left hand is next to the other rider's left hand. This is called riding left hand to left hand.

Left hands are next to each other as you pass.

When passing a horse that you do not know, or that is unpredictable, allow enough space in case it kicks.

THE SCHOOLING ARENA

Most of your work takes place in the schooling arena. Letters placed around the outside of the arena are used as guides for starting and finishing circles and other exercises called school figures. A standard arena is $65\frac{1}{2}$ ft x 131 ft (20 m x 40 m).

SCHOOL FIGURES

THE STANDARD ARENA	CIRCLES	CHANGING THE REIN
This standard arena is ideal for schooling exercises.	*The small circle is 33 ft (10 m) in diameter.*	*The figure eight enables you to change direction.*
The letters around the arena are always A, K, E, H, C, M, B, and F. Markers D, X, and G are placed along the center of the arena.	You can ride 66-ft (20-m) circles in a walk, trot, and canter from A, C, B, or E. Advanced horses and riders ride in smaller circles.	Turning across the schooling arena to change direction is called changing the rein. In this case it is practiced across the diagonal.

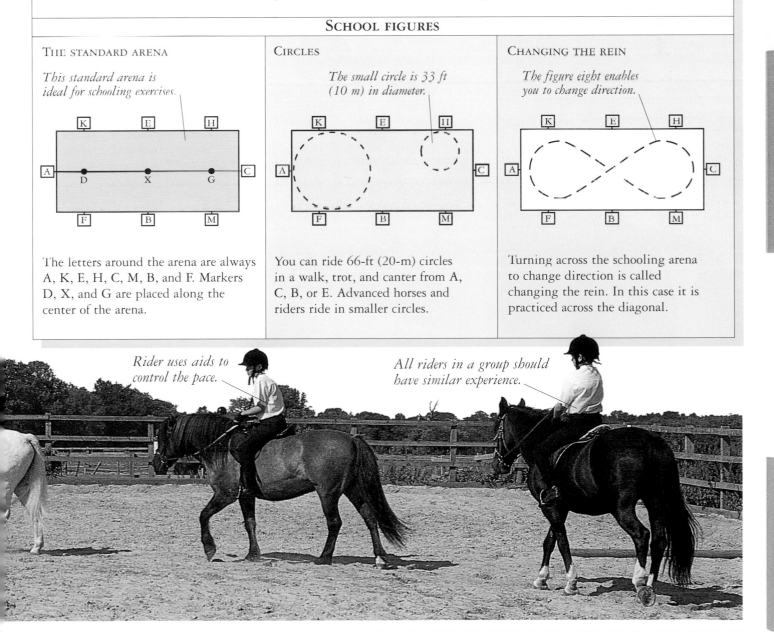

Rider uses aids to control the pace.

All riders in a group should have similar experience.

LEARNING TO JUMP

ONCE YOU CAN TROT and canter confidently, you can learn to jump. Before you start, you need to shorten your stirrups two or three holes so that you can stay in balance and follow your horse's movement. Always warm up before jumping so your horse is supple and obedient.

How a horse jumps

There are five phases to a jump – the approach, take-off, (suspension) in the air, landing, and departure. Keep your approach positive but calm, whether you are riding in trot or canter, and meet the fence straight. Look ahead and let your weight sink down to your heels.

Ground pole is at correct distance from fence for horse's stride length.

FIRST JUMP
Your first jump will be two poles in a low cross, approached from trot. A correctly placed pole on the ground in front, called a ground pole, helps you arrive at the correct takeoff point.

Knees act as shock absorbers.

Body weight should sink down through your legs into your heels.

Rider allows horse freedom of head and neck.

1 Takeoff
As the horse takes off, fold your upper body forward from the hips, and slide your hands far enough up the horse's neck to allow it freedom to stretch.

Horse pushes off with both back hooves.

2 In the air
Think about sliding your seat backward as you fold; do not stand up in the stirrups. As the horse's head and neck stretch forward and down, give slightly with the reins.

Trotting poles encourage horse to flex hocks.

TROTTING POLES
Poles spaced to allow one or more trot strides between them are called trotting poles. Use these to practice establishing a rhythmic stride and to introduce inexperienced horses to colored poles.

JUMPING PROBLEMS

If you are having problems, keep calm and go back to basics: perhaps your approach was hesitant or too fast. Never jump without a knowledgeable helper to advise you and alter fences. Always be ready to lower fences to make things easier and to restore the confidence of both you and your horse.

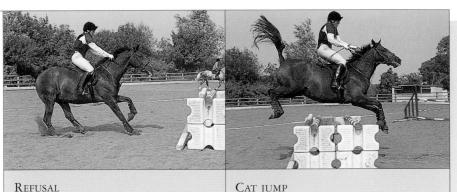

REFUSAL

A horse may stop in front of a fence or duck out to the side. This is called a refusal. A horse may refuse if the fence is too large or intimidating – if so adjust the fence. Ride straight at the fence with impulsion. You may have more control approaching at the trot.

CAT JUMP

A horse that jumps awkwardly instead of following a smooth arc through the air is said to cat jump. It usually happens when the horse takes off too close to the fence or is hesitant. To avoid this, try to establish a rhythm to the horse's strides and have impulsion.

Upper body becomes more upright.

Look up and ahead, either to your next fence or straight ahead if jumping a single fence.

Stirrup under widest part of foot

Light, unrestricting rein contact

3 Landing

As the horse lands, allow your upper body to become upright, without leaning back. Absorb landing impact through knees and ankles.

Horses should always wear protective boots.

Falling off

Everyone falls off occasionally, often because the horse or rider loses balance. Minimize the impact of falling by always wearing a hard hat or helmet and body protector. If you do fall, don't keep hold of the reins since the horse may step on you.

TRAIL RIDING

RIDING IN THE OPEN is called trail riding and is lots of fun. Horses enjoy trail rides and may be more lively than usual, so your trainer should make sure you are a confident, competent rider before taking you out. Most trail rides last for one or two hours and consist of a group of horses and riders. Before going on your first trail ride, make sure you know the rules of road safety, and that you have the right equipment.

Be aware of your horse's nature.

TRAIL HAZARDS
During a trail ride, you may have to cope with potential hazards, such as riding through water. If your horse is reluctant or nervous, keep calm and allow a confident horse and rider to go first. Following another horse's lead gives an inexperienced horse confidence.

Out and about
Before you leave the stable, always tell someone where you are going and when you expect to be back. When out, respect rights-of-way and ride slowly past farm animals and people. Canter only when the ground is suitable and when you can see far enough ahead.

The most experienced rider should set a pace that everyone can keep up with.

Check the girth before riding out.

SAFE TRAIL RIDES

The correct preparations and equipment will enable you to trail ride in safety and with enjoyment. Only experienced horses should be taken out alone. Never take out a horse that is nervous in traffic. Ride out only when you are feeling confident.

CHECKING BEFORE RIDE

CHECK TACK
Before you set out, it is important to check that your tack is in good condition and correctly fitted to the horse. Make sure your girth is tight enough and that all straps are fastened properly, with any loose ends pushed through the securing loops. There should be no wrinkles or folds in pads or cloths used underneath the saddle.

TACKING UP

CHECK SHOES
Pick out the horse's hooves with a hoofpick and be sure that all four shoes are in good condition. If a shoe is loose, the horse should not be ridden until the farrier has replaced it.

SAFETY EQUIPMENT

FLUORESCENT CLOTHING
Wearing fluorescent, reflective clothing in bad weather makes you more visible to other road users, especially drivers. Safety equipment includes belts and vests for riders, leg bands for horses, and lights that clip onto the stirrup irons.

SAFETY GEAR

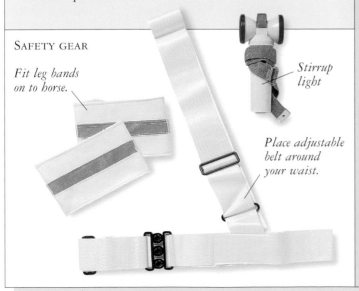

Fit leg bands on to horse.

Stirrup light

Place adjustable belt around your waist.

ROAD SAFETY

OBSERVATION
To ride out safely, be observant. Look ahead and behind before you move off, change direction, or pull out to move around parked cars or other hazards. At an intersection, stop and look in all directions, making sure it is safe before you proceed. Look ahead for things that may make your horse shy, such as roadwork, then check the road is free from traffic before riding past these obstacles. Never rely on your hearing – some cars are quiet and bicycles can't be heard. Stay on the side of the road, so other road users can pass you.

Remember to check behind as well as in front.

ROAD SENSE

HAND SIGNALS
Give hand signals before crossing roads or turning at intersections, and look both ahead and behind to make sure the road is clear before moving on. To turn right, hold your reins in your left hand and extend your right arm. To turn left, put the reins in your right hand and extend your left arm. Use the hand signals early enough and always ride on the same side as the traffic. Like motorists and cyclists, you must obey all road signs and traffic lights. Road users who don't realize they can frighten a horse will not warn you if they are near. Always thank drivers who slow down or wait.

Always look and signal before turning.

RIDING MANNERS

ADVANCED RIDING

WHEN YOU CAN RIDE confidently at all paces, you can learn more advanced movements. Your horse must already be trained to do these exercises, or it will not understand your aids. All the exercises shown here help make a horse more supple and balanced. They are useful for all forms of riding, as well as dressage.

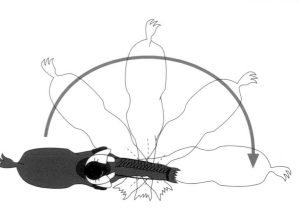

HOW A HORSE TURNS ON THE FOREHAND
As the horse looks to the right, the right hind leg crosses in front of the left one. At the same time, the horse pivots on its right foreleg. The horse should not move forward or backward.

Turning in place

This exercise is useful when opening gates. It is also the first step in teaching a horse to move sideways. When the horse moves its hindquarters around its front end, it is called a turn on the forehand. At first, ask for just a few steps.

2 Move sideways
Hold your left leg on the girth and pull gently on the left rein to ask the horse to move sideways, not forward or backward.

Rider must sit straight and must not pull back on the reins.

1 Begin turn
To turn to the right, squeeze your fingers on the right rein and put your right leg back to nudge the horse behind the girth.

Right hind leg crosses over in front of left.

Don't practice this exercise too often or for too long.

3 Using legs
Use your right leg in time with the horse's steps, not as a constant push. Practice this exercise in both directions by using the opposite rein and leg aids.

Rein back

When your horse can rein back, it is easier for you to open gates and maneuver in tight spaces. You will need to start this exercise from halt. Close both legs behind the girth; at the same time, close your fingers on the reins and sit lightly to tell the horse to step backward, not forward. You can teach a horse to rein back by asking a helper to press gently on its chest as you give the aids.

Horse and rider are in position to move backward.

Rider maintains contact on reins.

Steps should be calm and even, and horse should move in a straight line.

LATERAL WORK
Exercises in which a horse moves sideways and forward at the same time are called lateral work. These make a horse more obedient and supple. If you go sideways at too steep an angle, your horse will stop going forward.

Hands control energy and allow head and neck to stretch forward.

Rider's legs create energy.

EXTENDED PACES
An advanced horse will be able to perform extended walk, trot, and canter. This is when the horse's strides are as long as possible, but are not rushed. The first stage in achieving extension is to practice riding lengthened strides down the long side of the arena or across the diagonal. The rider must stay in balance with the horse's movement.

Horse's legs cross over as it moves forward and sideways.

ADVANCED JUMPING

ONCE YOU HAVE MASTERED the basics of jumping, you can enjoy challenges such as jumping courses and tackling cross-country fences. To improve your ability, your trainer will set up jumping exercises in which a certain number of strides are allowed between each fence. This is called gridwork. Practice fences should be low. Never jump without having someone there to help.

CROSS-COUNTRY
Cross-country courses are ridden at a faster canter than show-jumping courses and are set over distances of about 1–3 miles (1.6–4.8 km). Some fences, such as drop fences and some water jumps, should be approached at a trot.

Jumping a course

A novice show-jumping course has about 10 fences. Approach each fence straight on at an energetic but controlled pace, and make sure your horse always canters on the correct lead. If necessary, jump from a trot.

Look up and ahead, not down at the fence.

Allow the horse to stretch its head and neck forward as it jumps.

Protective boots should be put on a horse when jumping to minimize the risk of injury.

WARMING UP
Warm up over a single fence before jumping a whole course. Start with a cross pole, which is easy for the horse.

Gridwork

A grid is a row of fences spaced at set distances to allow the horse to take a certain number of strides between them. It helps train the horse into meeting each fence correctly so that you can concentrate on riding correctly. More difficult grids improve a horse's athletic ability. Always get help to adjust the fences.

Distances are set according to the length of your horse's stride.

Bounce jumps

Bounce fences make you and your horse more athletic. They are set so that the horse lands after the first jump and then immediately jumps over the second without taking any strides in between.

The horse should jump the small cross pole and land at a canter.

A basic grid can be used for novice horses and riders, or for warming up.

The first pole, on the ground, should be approached at a trot.

The horse should take two strides in a canter between fences.

The second cross pole is the same height as the first.

JUMPING DISTANCES

Distances between the two fences of a double are set according to a horse's size and stride length, and the type of jump used. The higher and wider the jump, the more room is needed. This chart shows some distances used between upright and parallel fences.

ONE NONJUMPING STRIDE			
HORSE HEIGHTS	TWO UPRIGHT FENCES	AN UPRIGHT THEN PARALLEL	TWO PARALLELS
Over 14.2 hh	24ft–26ft (7.30m–7.90m)	23ft 6in–25ft (7.15m–7.60m)	23ft–24ft (7m–7.30m)
14.2 hh	21ft 6in–24ft 6in (6.55m–7.45m)	21ft 6in–23ft 6in (6.55m–7.15m)	Not used
13.2 hh	20ft 6in–23ft (6.25m–7m)	Not used	Not used

TWO NONJUMPING STRIDES			
HORSE HEIGHTS	TWO UPRIGHT FENCES	AN UPRIGHT THEN PARALLEL	TWO PARALLELS
Over 14.2 hh	34ft 6in–36ft (10.50m–10.95m)	34ft 6in–35ft 6in (10.50m–10.80m)	34ft–35ft (10.35m–10.65m)
14.2 hh	31ft 6in–35ft (9.60m–10.65m)	31ft 6in–33ft 6in (9.60m–10.20m)	31ft 6in–33ft 6in (9.60m–10.20m)
13.2 hh	30ft–33ft 6in (9.15m–10.20m)	30ft–32ft 6in (9.15m–9.90m)	30ft–32ft 6in (9.15m–9.90m)

WESTERN RIDING

RIDING WESTERN STYLE, for pleasure and competition, is popular throughout the world. Western riders usually prefer to use curb bits or bitless bridles called hackamores. The reins are held loosely in one hand, and the rider steers by leaning the rein against the horse's neck. This is called neck reining.

This rider is wearing casual Western clothes; show clothes have elaborate details.

Saddling up

Western riding equipment is different from English-style tack. The bridle has no noseband and it usually has a curb bit and split reins. The saddle has a high front and back, and the girth is called a cinch.

The saddle blanket is made of heavy wool.

1 Put on bridle
Hold the bridle in front of the horse's face and slip the bit into its mouth. The split headstall (the top) goes around either side of the horse's ears.

2 Put on the blanket
The saddle blanket helps absorb sweat and prevent rubbing. Place it on the horse's back. This horse is trained to stand still when the reins are dropped to the ground.

3 Put on the saddle
Position the saddle on the horse's back, move the left stirrup out of the way, then tighten the latigo (front) and cinch (girth) straps.

Western training

A highly trained Western horse will turn on the spot, move sideways, or make a sliding stop from a flat-out gallop in response to light aids. A horse can be trained so that it may be ridden in both English and Western styles.

Riders of the Camargue, in France, ride in a style similar to that of Western riders and use similar saddles. They are called gardiens, and ride white Camargue stallions to herd the region's wild black bulls. Like Western horses, these horses are also trained to change direction quickly.

The ficheroun is a three-pronged pole used to control bulls.

Crupper helps keep saddle in place.

Place stirrup iron over saddle.

Cinch strap

Food supplies are carried in the saddlebags.

Bedroll may have a waterproof cover.

Lariat for roping cattle is attached to the saddle horn.

4 **Ready to go**
A working cowboy's horse must carry all his equipment, including a bedroll.

TRAINING A HORSE

AN EXPERIENCED RIDER may be able to help train young or inexperienced horses. Training is enjoyable and rewarding, but must always be supervised by an expert. Practice skills such as long reining with an older, experienced horse before helping to teach a young one. Ride out a young horse in the company of a sensible horse and rider to boost the horse's confidence before taking it out alone.

Early lessons

Lunging and long reining teach a horse to obey voice commands. Long reining, where the trainer is positioned behind the horse, teaches it to stop, start, and turn and to accept the feel of a bit. This means that when a rider mounts the horse for the first time, the horse already understands some of the basic aids. Start by long reining in a safe, enclosed area.

Hard hat or helmet should always be worn when working young horses.

Riding boots are the safest footwear since they will not slip.

Gloves prevent injury if the reins are pulled through your hands.

USING LONG REINS
Long reins may frighten a horse when used for the first time. Before going outside, introduce the reins in the stable so that the horse is used to feeling them around its legs. When using the long reins, remember to use voice commands at the same time.

Long reins

Coil the long reins safely out of the way.

Rider is given leg up to lean over.

Handler holds and reassures horse.

Always wear a body protector.

MOUNTING A YOUNG HORSE

Teaching a horse to accept a rider is challenging. First the rider leans over the saddle so that the horse gets used to the weight. When the horse is comfortable with the weight, the rider places one foot in the stirrup and swings the other leg over the saddle. Riding horses should not be ridden until they are three years old.

HELP FROM AN EXPERT

Introduce a horse to new skills, such as jumping, with expert help. A trainer will assess the horse's reaction to new experiences and decide when to progress to the next stage. Keep the first lessons short, and always finish on a good note so the horse stays relaxed.

Long reins attach to the bit.

Keep a light hold on the long reins and squeeze them gently to stop or turn.

Long reins pass through shortened stirrups.

Protective boots should be worn by horse for all training work.

DIFFICULT PONIES

YOU MAY COME ACROSS PONIES that are difficult to ride or handle and that have specific behavioral problems. Never try to solve these problems alone – get help from an experienced adult. The expert should always start by checking that the pony is not uncomfortable or in pain, since this causes many problems. Ask your vet's advice if necessary, and get an expert to check the fit of your tack. Too much high-energy food and too little exercise will cause hyperactive or bad behavior.

An experienced rider will not be thrown off the pony.

Check that saddle does not pinch.

EXPERT HELP
If a pony starts to misbehave, ask your trainer to check its teeth, tack, and feeding routine. Any problems should be corrected and the pony should be ridden by an experienced, confident rider until it settles down.

Difficult temperaments

Healthy ponies that have been trained and handled correctly should be confident and friendly. Ponies that have had rushed or incorrect training sessions, or those that have had bad experiences, may be nervous or stubborn. Naturally aggressive ponies are rare, but some may bite or kick to prevent you from doing something they dislike.

When a pony's ears are laid back it is confused or frightened.

Male horses and ponies, called stallions, may rear up onto their hind legs to fight, and they may use their teeth and forelegs.

AGGRESSIVE PONIES
Horses and ponies are sometimes aggressive with each other, but rarely attack people. Some kick or bite if previous rough handling has caused them pain. Do not try to separate ponies that are fighting in the field since you may get hurt.

NERVOUS PONIES
A pony may be generally nervous, or worried about particular things, such as traffic. It must be handled in a quiet and confident manner and ridden by an expert. Never go for a trail ride on a traffic-shy pony. It must be retrained by an experienced professional.

COMMON PROBLEMS

All ponies misbehave occasionally and even the quietest ones may buck, rear, shy, or bolt if startled. Problems occur when bad behavior becomes a habit. An out-of-control pony is too dangerous for anyone but an expert to deal with.

RIDING PROBLEMS

BOLTING
A bolting pony runs off in a panic, and ignores its rider's signals to stop. Never ride a pony that is known to bolt. If a pony gallops off when you are already riding it, slow down by pulling and slackening the reins repeatedly; do not pull the reins continuously. Use your voice to reassure the pony.

SHYING
A shying pony may jump sideways if something frightens it. If you spot something that your pony might shy at, turn its head slightly away from the hazard, and look ahead as you ride past. Use your legs to keep a pony moving and try not to tense up since the pony will sense that you are nervous.

A REARING PONY

The pony must learn that it cannot get its own way by rearing.

REARING
If a pony rears while you are riding, lean forward and do not pull back on the reins. If you do, the pony may fall over backward. As the pony brings its feet back to the ground, ride forward with determination.

PULLING
If a pony pulls, have its teeth checked and make sure that its bit fits correctly. Get expert advice to find out if you need to use a different bit or noseband. Practice riding between a walk and a trot in the riding arena, using your voice as well as other aids. While doing this, give and take on the reins – don't just pull on them.

DIFFICULT TO MOUNT
If a pony is difficult to mount, ask someone to stand at the pony's head and hold the bridle. Use a mounting block instead of mounting from the ground, so there is no chance of the saddle being pulled over. Be careful not to dig your toe into a pony's ribs as you get on.

HANDLING PROBLEMS

PULLS WHEN LED
If your pony pulls, practice leading it in an enclosed area and make sure it understands your voice commands. Use a bridle, or a training halter that applies pressure when a pony pulls, and slackens when it stops pulling. When leading, pull and then slacken the reins or halter; do not pull constantly.

A pony should come when you show it food.

DIFFICULT TO CATCH

RUSHES OUT OF THE STABLE
Make sure the stable doorway is not too narrow – if a pony has banged against it at some time, it may rush out through fear. Use a bridle or training halter to give you more control. Reward a pony for good behavior, and practice until it has gained confidence.

DIFFICULT TO LOAD
The trailer must be light and inviting, with a safe, stable ramp. Allow plenty of time to practice when loading. Put protective leg wraps on the pony and wear a hat, safe boots, and gloves yourself. Some ponies gain confidence from following an experienced one. Don't give up!

DIFFICULT TO CATCH
Leave a leather or safety halter on a pony that is difficult to catch. Reward it with food when it comes to you. Catch the pony regularly, reward it, and then release it immediately so it does not think that coming to you always means work. Catch other ponies first, so that the pony has no friends left in the field.

KICKING
Never stand directly behind a pony, whether it kicks or not. If a pony is prone to kicking, try to find out why it kicks. Problems are often caused when girths are tightened too roughly. If this is not the case and it still kicks, speak sharply to the pony. Keep ponies that kick other ponies at a safe distance when being ridden.

RIDING VACATIONS

THERE ARE RIDING vacations to suit all ages and abilities, from treks or trail rides in different countries to camps where you can improve your riding and horse care skills or try different activities. You can choose whether you ride lots of different ponies, or look after one as if it was your own.

Trained instructors will look after you each day.

EDUCATIONAL TRIPS
If you do not own a pony, you may enjoy visiting a riding vacation stable for a week or two where you can ride every day and help look after the ponies. As well as lessons, you may be able to take part in shows and other activities, such as picnic or beach rides.

Vacation packages

When choosing a vacation, be honest about your ability and experience. This will help the organizers to give you a pony you will enjoy riding. If you do not feel happy riding the pony allocated to you, tell the trainer or ride leader. Riding vacations are a great way of making new friends with the same interests and having lots of fun at the same time.

A waterproof jacket and gloves must be taken in case weather conditions are bad.

Always take your hard hat or helmet with you on a trip.

Check all tack has been fitted correctly and that the pony is comfortable before you go out for a ride.

Ride sensibly and be aware of anything that may startle your pony.

SPECIAL-INTEREST VACATIONS
If you are confident in basic riding skills, you may want to try a vacation where you can specialize in a particular activity, such as dressage or jumping. Alternatively, you could try something different, such as Western riding. The stable should have experienced and well-trained horses and ponies. Many dude ranches and vacation stables offer complete packages.

Horses must be well trained and experienced.

Treks and trail rides

Long rides, called treks or trail rides, give you the chance to explore interesting areas on surefooted horses. Your trip may take you along mountain paths or across terrain that could not be reached on short rides. These types of vacations can be found all over the world.

Enjoy the spectacular scenery and interesting wildlife during your trek.

You need to be in good shape before embarking on a trek.

FIRST AID AND SAFETY

TO RIDE SAFELY means preparing well, choosing the right clothes and equipment, and knowing what to do in an emergency. Always check that the pony's shoes and tack are in good condition, and never use damaged equipment. Learn the basics of first aid for both horses and people. This will help you to stay calm in an emergency when others may need your help.

Bag containing essentials can be fastened around the rider's waist.

FIRST-AID KIT
One rider in a group should carry a basic first-aid kit. This should include a hoofpick in case a pony gets a stone lodged in its hoof. If available, take a cell phone – switched off – for emergencies.

Riding out safely
Before leaving the stable always tell someone where you are going and when you will be back. If you are riding a pony for the first time, go out with a friend whose pony is quiet and reliable. Take trail rides in daylight only, and do not gallop on verges or pedestrian rights of way.

Hat cover is made from fluorescent, reflective material

Tack should be in good condition, particularly stitching on the reins, girths, and stirrup leathers.

Always ride on the correct side of the road, facing oncoming traffic.

BEING SEEN
Make sure that other road users can see you from as far away as possible, so that they have a chance to slow down and pass safely. Wear fluorescent, reflective clothing, such as vests and hat covers, on overcast or rainy days. This is a sensible precaution to take in all weather conditions on busy roads.

Keep calm and reassure the rider, then have someone call emergency services.

Emergency first aid

If you witness a riding accident, try to prevent an injured rider from getting up. If the rider is unconscious, check his or her breathing and clear the air passages if necessary. Do not remove the rider's hat – a possible neck or back injury may be made worse. If the rider seems dazed or confused, he or she may have a concussion. Place the rider in the recovery position and call for help.

The recovery position is the safest position in which to place an injured person.

Stay with the injured rider until emergency services arrive.

Do not attempt to remove boots.

Cover the rider with a blanket if he or she feels cold.

Attending to horse injury

You may need to attend to an injured horse when you are out for a ride. If a fracture is suspected, keep the horse still and call the vet immediately. If blood is spurting from a wound, a main artery has probably been severed. Apply a clean pressure pad to minimize bleeding and call the vet.

1 Dress the wound

Gently clip hair from the edges of the wound and wash away any dirt with clean water. Place a sterile, nonstick dressing with padding over the wound.

Place padding over the dressing before using a bandage.

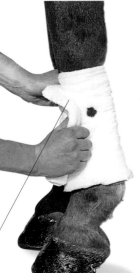

2 Secure the padding

Keep the padding in place with a self-adhesive bandage. Keep pressure even, but do not pull the bandage too tight.

Start at the top to secure padding, then move down to wound area.

Hold the leg firmly with one hand.

3 Finish up

Bandage the leg so that you leave an edge of padding at the top and bottom. Change the dressings twice a day to prevent the wound from becoming infected.

OWNING OR SHARING A PONY

Everyone who loves ponies dreams of owning one or, if that's not possible, sharing someone else's. Before having a pony of your own, you must develop the necessary riding and horse handling skills. This chart explains the skills you need.

HANDLING SKILLS

TACKING UP AND UNTACKING

Make sure you tack up and untack in safe surroundings so that the pony stays under control. Put the bridle on first, placing the reins over the pony's head in case it tries to walk off. Be aware of the pony's comfort; don't bang the bit against its teeth or pull up the girth suddenly. Learn how to adjust tack correctly and how to recognize whether a saddle fits well. Store tack in a safe, dry place.

PUTTING ON A BRIDLE

After riding, remember to clean tack thoroughly.

GROOMING

Learn the names and uses of all the grooming tools and keep separate items for each pony. Before you groom, tie up the pony safely. Use a separate sponge for eyes, nose, and dock. Use a hoof pick to pick out the hoof from heel to toe. Wash the brushes and stable cloths regularly. The best time to groom a pony is after exercise when the skin is warm and the pony is relaxed.

BLANKETING

Learn about the different needs of a pasture-kept pony and a stabled pony. Find out about the merits of different types of blankets, and how to fit and adjust them so that the pony is protected and comfortable. Remember to use a blanket when a pony has just been clipped. Keep blankets clean and have spare blankets in case one gets damaged.

PUTTING ON A BLANKET

Practice putting on a blanket so that it fits correctly.

LEADING INTO A TRAILER

PREPARE FOR TRAVEL

Practice putting on and removing traveling equipment, including a tail bandage and traveling boots. Remember that a vehicle must be bright and inviting, so that the pony is happy to walk into it; the ramp must be safe and steady. Practice leading a pony straight up the ramp, tying it up inside the vehicle, then leading it out again. Be aware of safety precautions, and wear a hard hat and protective footwear when loading a pony.

RIDING SKILLS

FIRST STEPS
Learn to mount and dismount safely and to hold the reins correctly. Practice tightening the girth and adjusting the stirrup leathers while mounted. Understand the natural aids – the legs, voice, hands, and seat – and how to use them to stop, start, and turn the pony. Practice exercises in and out of the saddle to increase your suppleness.

ON A HACK

Ride sensibly and be prepared for any hazards.

TROTTING
Practice the rising and sitting trot without bumping. Remember to let the pony's movement push you out of the saddle when rising, and to absorb the movement through your lower back when sitting. Learn to feel each diagonal without looking at the pony's legs. Practice riding from a walk to a trot, and then halt.

CANTERING
Recognize which foreleg is the leading leg (the one that takes the longer stride). Remember that on a circle or bend, the inside leg (nearest the center) should lead. Practice absorbing the horse's movement through your lower back. Know how to change your seat when galloping.

JUMPING
Make sure you can control a pony's speed and direction when trotting and cantering, and can ride transitions between all gaits. Ask your instructor to check your jumping position and to help you ride over trotting poles and small jumping grids. Practice jumping courses over small fences.

TRAIL RIDING
To gain confidence, ride out on a quiet pony, with other riders. Know how to ride safely on the road. Adjust your balance when riding up and down steep hills (or slopes) – bend your upper body forward from the hips going uphill, and sit upright downhill.

SAFETY AND CARE SKILLS

WHEN TO CALL THE VET
Recognize signs that may mean the pony is ill, such as listlessness. Learn how to spot colic or laminitis. Be confident about taking a pony's temperature, pulse, and respiration rates. Learn how to trot up a pony to check for lameness, and how to tell which leg is lame. Call the vet if you are worried.

TROTTING UP A HORSE
Trot the horse on a hard, level surface.

ROAD SAFETY
Understand the importance of using hand signals on the road and wearing bright clothing. Learn how to give hand signals to show that you wish to turn left or right, and to request other road users to slow down or stop. Always ride on the correct side of the road so that you are facing oncoming traffic.

SHOEING
Ask your stable farrier to show you the points of a well-shod hoof. Remember that all ponies should have their hooves trimmed every six weeks, even if they are not being ridden or do not wear shoes. Ask your farrier to explain how studs are fitted to shoes and when they should be used. Practice picking out a pony's hooves.

BASIC FIRST AID
You should know what a first-aid kit for a pony contains. Know how to deal with minor wounds and how to apply dressings and bandages correctly. Keep a first-aid kit in case a rider is injured. Learn how to put an injured rider in the recovery position and remember not to remove an injured rider's hat. Understand how to call for emergency services.

FEEDING
Understand the basic rules of feeding and always make sure that forage makes up at least half of each day's food. Learn how to calculate how much food a pony needs according to its weight, workload, age, and type. Recognize different types of feed and learn how to fill and tie up a haynet and clean out a stable. Make sure clean water is always available.

GLOSSARY

THERE ARE MANY words used specifically to describe horses, their equipment, and the way that we ride and train them. Some have been used throughout this book and can be found, with a description of their meaning, below.

AIDS Signals used to communicate with and give instructions to a horse or pony. Natural aids are the legs, seat, hands, and voice.

BACKING Teaching a young horse or pony to accept a rider.

CANTER A three-beat gait that is faster than a walk and a trot, but slower than a gallop.

CHANGING THE DIAGONAL Sitting for one beat of a trot, then rising again to adjust the way a horse or pony carries the rider's weight.

CROSS SURCINGLES Crossed straps that fasten underneath a horse's or pony's belly and hold a blanket in place.

EXTENDED STRIDES Action in which a horse or pony takes strides that are as long as possible, without hurrying. Can be in a walk, trot, or canter.

FORAGE Grass and hay, which should form at least half of the total amount of food a horse or pony eats each day.

FOREHAND The front end of a horse or pony – its head, neck, shoulders, and forelegs.

GALLOP A four-beat gait, the fastest pace of all.

GRID A line of fences, spaced at set distances, so a horse or pony meets each one at the correct takeoff point. Schooling over a grid is called gridwork.

HAND SIGNALS Signals given with the hands and arms to indicate which way a rider intends to turn when riding on the roads.

INDOOR ARENA Covered building where horses or ponies are trained or riding lessons are given.

JODHPURS Special pants worn by riders, with reinforced leg patches and specially designed seams.

LATERAL WORK Exercises in which the horse moves forward and sideways.

LEADING LEG In a canter, a horse or pony takes a longer stride with one foreleg, called the leading leg, than the other.

LONG REINING Method of training a young horse or pony to stop, start, and turn before it is ready to accept a rider.

LUNGING 1. Method of training a horse or pony to accept voice commands. 2. Method where a trainer controls a horse or pony during early lessons so the novice rider can concentrate on his or her riding techniques.

MARTINGALE A piece of tack used to prevent a horse or pony from raising its head too high.

NECK REINING Method of turning a horse or pony, used by Western riders.

REIN BACK Advanced movement where a horse or pony steps back in a straight line.

RISING TROT Where the rider is alternately pushed out of the saddle by a horse's or pony's movement for one beat, then sits for the next.

SADDLE PAD A thick wool blanket used under a Western saddle to prevent sores.

SCHOOLING ARENA An enclosed area used for riding exercises. Sometimes called a manege.

SHYING When a horse or pony swerves sideways away from an object or from noise.

SIDE REINS Reins used to control a horse's or pony's head carriage while it is being lunged.

SITTING TROT The rider does not rise, but sits and absorbs a horse's or pony's movement through the lower back.

TACKING UP Putting on a horse's saddle and bridle. Untacking is taking off the saddle and bridle.

TRAIL RIDING Riding in the open, either on road and tracks or across open countryside.

TRANSITION The passage from one gait to another. Transitions should be smooth, and a horse or pony should stay in balance.

TROT A two-beat gait in which legs move in diagonal pairs. It is faster than a walk, but slower than a canter.

TURN ON THE FOREHAND An exercise where a horse or pony stays in one spot and moves its hindquarters around its front end (forehand).

WESTERN RIDING The American style of riding. The reins are held in one hand, the stirrups are long, and the saddle is very deep.

INDEX

EXERCISES IN
THE SADDLE

ACKNOWLEDGMENTS

Dorling Kindersley would like to thank the following people whose assistance have made the preparation of this book possible.

The author
Carolyn Henderson has lived and worked with horses for many years. She is a regular contributor to special interest magazines such as *Horse and Hound*, and has written and edited a variety of books on all aspects of keeping, riding, and training horses.

The publishers would also like to thank the following: Hilary Bird for the index and Cheryl Telfer for additional design.

CAM Equestrian Ltd, Eardisley, Hereford for providing images of jumping poles. Lethers, Merstham, Surrey for the loan of equipment and tack. Jackki Garnham and staff and riders, Beechwood Riding School, Woldingham, Surrey; Sandra Waylett, Gatton Park Livery, Reigate, Surrey; Ebbisham Farm Livery Stables,

Walton on the Hill, Surrey, for use of their facilities. The models Holly Clarke, Rosie Eustace, Emma de la Mothe, Kerry Meade, Alison Forrest, and Samantha Wilkinson.
Also thanks to the horses and ponies used in photography and their owners for loaning them. These are: *Cinnamon Dust* (owned by Holly Clarke); *Ginger Pick* (owned by Sandra Waylett); *Blondie* and *Tikki* (owned by Jakki Garnham); *Face the Music* (in care of Carolyn Henderson); *Sparkie* (owned by Kerry Meade).

Every effort has been made to adhere to latest safety standards in the making of this book.

Picture Credits
The publishers would like to thank the following people for their kind permission to reproduce their photographs.

key: *b* bottom, *c* center, *l* left, *t* top, *r* right

Robert Harding Picture Library: 40*t*; **Kit Houghton**: 2;

8*t*; 9; 37*tr*; 38*t*; 41*t*; 42*b*; **Bob Langrish**: 28*t*; 32*t*; 33*t*; 37*tl*; 38*bl*; 40*b*; 45*b*; **Pictor International**: 35*tl*; **Tony Stone Images**: 38*br*; 41*b* (David Hiser).

Additional photography
Other photography was taken by: **Geoff Brightling**: 34*tr*, *tl*; 34-35; 35*br*, *tl;* **Kit Houghton**: 17*tl*, *tc*; 19*tl*, *tc*, *tr*; 23*cl*, *cc*, *cr;* **Bob Langrish**: 28*b*; 29*tl*; *tr*, *br*, 6-7; 45*t*; 26*l*; 26-27; 27*r*; *tc*, *tr;* **Tim Ridley**: 29*bl*.

Useful addresses
Here are the addresses of some associations that you may want to contact:

American Riding Instructors Association
28801 Trenton Court
Bonita Springs
FL 34134-3337
Tel: (239) 948-3232
Fax: (239) 948-5053

American Horse Shows Association
4047 Iron Works Parkway
Lexington, KY 40511
Tel: (859) 258-2472
Fax: (859) 231-6662
Website: www.usef.org

American Youth Horse Council
577 N. Boyero Avenue
Pueblo West, CO 81007
Tel: (719) 594-9778
E-mail info@ayhc.com

Horsemanship Safety Association Inc.
517 Bear Road
Lake Placid,
FL 33852
Tel: (941) 465-0289
Fax: (800) 798-8106
E-mail: HSANews@aol.com

North American Riding for the Handicapped Association
P.O. Box 33150
Denver,
CO 80233
Tel: (303) 369-RIDE
Email: NARHA@NARHA.org

United States Pony Clubs Inc.
4041 Iron Works Parkway
Lexington,
KY 40511
Tel: (859) 254-7669
Fax: (859) 233-4652
Website: www.ponyclub.org